I0151821

SUMMARY OF THE SPIRIT REALM

The Place We Work with God in Prayer

PATSY CAMENETI

Harrison House

Copyright 2024–Harrison House

All rights reserved. This book is protected by the copyright laws of the United States of America. This book may not be copied or reprinted for commercial gain or profit. The use of short quotations or occasional page copying for personal or group study is permitted and encouraged. Permission will be granted upon request. Unless otherwise indicated, all scripture quotations are taken from the *King James Version* of the Bible. Used by permission. All rights reserved.

All emphasis within Scripture quotations is the author's own. Please note that Harrison House's publishing style capitalizes certain pronouns in Scripture that refer to the Father, Son, and Holy Spirit, and may differ from some publishers' styles. Take note that the name satan and related names are not capitalized. We choose not to acknowledge him, even to the point of violating grammatical rules.

Harrison House P.O. Box 310, Shippensburg, PA 17257-0310

This book and all other Harrison House's books are available at Christian bookstores and distributors worldwide.

For Worldwide Distribution.

Reach us on the Internet: www.harrisonhouse.com.

ISBN 13 TP: 9781667508641

ISBN 13 eBook: 9781667508658

CONTENTS

INTRODUCTION

꧁꧂

Summary of "The Spirit Realm"

In "The Spirit Realm," we explore the unseen but profoundly influential dimensions of existence beyond the physical world. This summary delves into the book's key insights and teachings on understanding and interacting with the spiritual realm. It covers various topics, including the nature of spiritual beings, the significance of spiritual warfare, the power of prayer, and the roles of faith and divine guidance in navigating the unseen.

As you read this summary, you will gain a clearer understanding of how the spirit realm intersects with our daily lives and how we, as believers, can effectively engage with it to fulfill God's purposes. Whether you are a seasoned spiritual warrior or new to the concept of spiritual realities, this summary will provide you with valuable perspectives and practical guidance for your spiritual journey.

Chapter Highlights:

• **The Reality of the Spirit Realm:** Unveiling the existence and characteristics of the spiritual dimension.

• **Angels and Demons:** Understanding the roles, purposes, and activities of both heavenly and fallen beings.

• **Spiritual Warfare:** Equipping yourself with the knowledge and tools needed to combat spiritual forces.

• **The Power of Prayer:** Harnessing the transformative power of prayer to influence the spiritual realm.

• **Faith and Divine Guidance:** Learning to trust and follow divine direction in all aspects of life.

• **God's Sovereignty and Our Role:** Recognizing how God's ultimate plan is carried out through our partnership with Him.

Each chapter offers profound insights, scriptural references, and real-life examples to illuminate the dynamic interaction between the seen and unseen worlds. As you journey through this summary, be prepared to deepen your spiritual awareness and strengthen your relationship with God, empowering you to walk confidently and victoriously in both realms.

CHAPTER 1

AN INVITATION TO WORK WITH GOD

Bible Verse

"I am the true grapevine, and my Father is the gardener. He cuts off every branch of mine that doesn't produce fruit, and he prunes the branches that do bear fruit so they will produce even more." - John 15:1-2 (NLT)

Introduction

This chapter reveals a dream where the author learns a profound lesson about working with God rather than independently. It explores the importance of aligning our efforts and prayers with God's will and guidance, highlighting the pitfalls of self-assignment in spiritual endeavors.

Word of Wisdom

"My best energies in prayer were absolutely nothing if they were discon-

nected from His direction and in-
spiration."

Main Theme

The chapter emphasizes the necessity of collaborating with God in prayer and spiritual work, ensuring that our actions are driven by divine inspiration rather than personal zeal.

Key Points

- The author had a dream where Jesus performed surgery, illustrating the futility of self-assigned tasks.
- The dream highlighted the importance of following God's assignments rather than self-imposing responsibilities.
- The author recognized their prayers had become self-driven rather than Spirit-led.
- Jesus' teachings from John 5:19 and John 15:4-5 emphasize the need for divine connection.
- The author learned the value of abiding in Jesus to bear true spiritual fruit.
- Prayer should be an extension of God's will and desires, not merely personal efforts.

Key Themes

- **Divine Assignment vs. Self-Assignment:** The author realized that their involvement in a person's life was self-imposed and not divinely assigned, leading to ineffective efforts. True spiritual work requires God's direction and assignment.

- **Dependence on God:** The dream underscored the necessity of being dependent on God's guidance. Just as Jesus depended on His Father, believers must rely on God for fruitful endeavors.
- **Abiding in the Vine:** The chapter expounds on John 15:4-5, illustrating that fruitful spiritual life comes from abiding in Jesus, the Vine. Without this connection, efforts remain fruitless.
- **Spirit-Led Prayer:** Effective prayer aligns with God's will and is inspired by the Holy Spirit. The author reflects on their previous prayers and the lack of divine inspiration behind them.
- **Collaborative Work with God:** Working with God means being an extension of His will and desire on earth. When believers are in sync with God's will, their prayers and actions become powerful and effective.

Conclusion

The chapter calls readers to reflect on their spiritual practices, ensuring that their efforts are aligned with God's will and direction. It encourages a shift from self-assigned tasks to Spirit-led actions, fostering a deeper connection with God and more effective prayer life. Through abiding in Jesus and being directed by the Holy Spirit, believers can truly work with God and bear abundant fruit.

CHAPTER 2

THE MINISTRY OF PRAYER

Bible Verse

"God is faithful (reliable, trustworthy, and therefore ever true to His promise, and He can be depended on); by Him you were called into companionship and participation with His Son, Jesus Christ our Lord." - 1 Corinthians 1:9 (AMPC)

Introduction

T his chapter reflects on the author's early job experiences and draws a parallel to their spiritual journey, emphasizing the importance of knowing and working with God rather than merely for Him. It illustrates how prayer can be a ministry where believers align with God's will, serving as effective partners in His work.

Word of Wisdom

"Obedience is better than sacrifice."

• • •

Main Theme

The chapter underscores the significance of developing a personal relationship with God in the ministry of prayer, working with Him to fulfill His divine purposes rather than relying on self-directed efforts.

Key Points

- The author's first job in a flower shop taught them the value of working closely with the employer.
- The second job as a nurse's aide lacked personal connection, illustrating a different work dynamic.
- These experiences parallel the difference between working for God and working with God.
- True ministry involves companionship and participation with Jesus.
- Effective prayer is driven by God's will and inspiration, not personal zeal.
- Epaphras serves as a biblical example of earnest, Spirit-led prayer ministry.

Key Themes

- **Personal Relationship with God:** The author emphasizes that knowing and working closely with God, like their first job, is crucial for effective ministry. This personal connection is essential for understanding and carrying out God's will.
- **Difference Between Working For and With God:** The chapter highlights the distinction between working for God in a detached manner and working with Him in close collaboration. The latter is more effective and fulfilling.
- **Prayer as Ministry:** The ministry of prayer is portrayed as a vital way to work with God, where believers participate in His plans and purposes. This requires a deep connection with God and reliance on His guidance.
- **Epaphras' Example:** The chapter cites Epaphras as a model of earnest and Spirit-led prayer. His dedication and fervent prayers for the church exemplify how believers can serve God through intercession.
- **Obedience and Divine Alignment:** The author stresses the importance of obedience to God's instructions over personal sacrifices or self-directed efforts. Aligning with God's will ensures that prayer and ministry are effective and fruitful.

Conclusion

The chapter encourages readers to cultivate a close, personal relationship with God to become effective partners in His ministry. By aligning their prayers and actions with God's will, believers can participate in His divine work, much like a skilled surgical team following the lead of a surgeon. This approach transforms prayer into a powerful ministry, enabling believers to fulfill their role in God's kingdom with greater impact and fulfillment.

CHAPTER 3

GOD IS A SPIRIT

Bible Verse

"God is Spirit, and those who worship Him must worship in spirit and truth." - John 4:24 (NKJV)

Introduction

This chapter explores the concept of working with God in the ministry of prayer by understanding that God is a Spirit. It emphasizes that effective prayer requires a spiritual connection with God, transcending mere religious routines or rituals.

Word of Wisdom

"God isn't McDonald's. He's not Amazon. He's not a corporation, and He's definitely not a robot. He is a Spirit. He can be known and loved."

Main Theme

The chapter underscores the necessity of recognizing God's spiritual nature and engaging with Him accordingly, particularly in the ministry of prayer, which calls for a deep, personal connection.

Key Points

- Jesus emphasized that God is a Spirit, highlighting the importance of spiritual interaction.
- Effective prayer involves engaging with God in spirit and truth, beyond physical senses.
- Knowing God's will and praying with confidence is essential for receiving answers.
- The Word of God provides a solid foundation for prayer.
- Superficial prayer practices, likened to ordering from McDonald's or Amazon, lack true engagement with God.
- Intimate fellowship with God is crucial for a transformative prayer life.

Key Themes

- **Spiritual Engagement in Prayer:** Prayer should transcend physical senses and be rooted in spiritual interaction. Recognizing God as a Spirit requires believers to engage with Him in spirit and truth, which enhances the effectiveness of their prayers.

- **Confidence in God's Will:** Praying with the confidence that comes from knowing God's will is fundamental. This confidence is derived from faith and a deep understanding of God's Word, ensuring that prayers align with His purposes.
- **Avoiding Superficial Prayer:** The chapter warns against treating prayer like a transaction, similar to ordering from McDonald's or Amazon. Such an approach lacks the depth and intimacy required for a meaningful relationship with God.
- **Importance of Fellowship:** The chapter highlights the significance of intimate fellowship with God. Examples from the Bible, such as Enoch's close walk with God, demonstrate the profound impact of a deep spiritual connection.
- **Universal Invitation to Fellowship:** The promise of fellowship with God is extended to all believers. Hebrews 11:5-6 underscores that anyone who sincerely seeks God can experience this close relationship, provided they believe in His existence and seek Him earnestly.

Conclusion

The chapter calls readers to deepen their understanding of God as a Spirit and to cultivate a more intimate and spiritual approach to prayer. By recognizing the importance of engaging with God in spirit and truth, believers can transform their prayer lives, aligning their wills with God's purposes and experiencing a more profound connection with Him. This spiritual intimacy is the key to effective and fulfilling ministry in prayer.

CHAPTER 4

COME TO ME

Bible Verse

"Let us then approach God's throne of grace with confidence, so that we may receive mercy and find grace to help us in our time of need." - Hebrews 4:16 (NIV)

Introduction

This chapter emphasizes God's strong desire for us to come to Him, highlighting the ways we can respond to His invitation. It explores the scriptural basis for drawing near to God and provides practical ways to foster a deeper relationship with Him.

Word of Wisdom

"Because of the great provision from God through Jesus' blood, let's not let anything keep us from coming and drawing near to God."

. . .

Main Theme

The chapter underscores the importance of accepting God's invitation to draw near to Him, offering practical steps to develop a close and fruitful relationship through various spiritual practices.

Key Points

- God's desire for us to come to Him is even stronger than our longing for His presence.
- The tabernacle and sacrifices were God's idea to facilitate closeness with Him.
- Jesus' first coming was to make a way for us to access God freely.
- Coming to God today requires shifting our attention to Him, not a physical journey.
- Scripture consistently invites all to come to God, promising rewards for those who seek Him.
- Practical ways to come to God include prioritizing His Word, worship, and prayer.

Key Themes

- **God's Strong Desire for Relationship:** God's longing for a relationship with us is profound, as evidenced by the establishment of the tabernacle and sacrifices. His ultimate demonstration of this desire was sending Jesus to provide a way for us to come to Him freely.

- **Accessibility Through Jesus' Sacrifice:** Jesus' blood made it possible for us to come boldly to God, removing any barriers. This accessibility is a cornerstone of our relationship with God, allowing us to approach Him with confidence.
- **Practical Ways to Draw Near:** The chapter outlines seven practical ways to draw near to God, emphasizing that these actions are not to earn His favor but to accept His invitation. These practices include putting God's Word first, worshiping, and praying in tongues.
- **Handling Sin and Worries:** Sin and worries can be transformed into opportunities to draw closer to God by approaching Him boldly for mercy and grace. This perspective shifts these potentially negative experiences into moments of deeper fellowship with God.
- **Continual Invitation:** God's invitation to come to Him is ongoing and applies to everyone, regardless of their current spiritual state. This open invitation is a testament to His love and desire for a close relationship with each of us.

Conclusion

The chapter calls readers to embrace God's invitation to come to Him in various aspects of their lives. By prioritizing His Word, engaging in heartfelt worship, and confidently approaching

Him with their needs and confessions, believers can cultivate a deeper, more fulfilling relationship with God. This ongoing interaction transforms their spiritual lives, making them more aware of His presence and guidance.

❦

CHAPTER 5

YOU ARE A SPIRIT

Bible Verse

"Blessed are you who hunger now, for you shall be filled." -
Luke 6:21 (NKJV)

Introduction

This chapter explores the remarkable concept that humans, created as spirits, can engage in ongoing conversations and interactions with God, who is a Spirit. It delves into the spiritual capabilities inherent in every human and emphasizes the importance of being spiritually aware to effectively work with God.

Word of Wisdom

"Our goal is to know Jesus and to work together with Him."

Main Theme

The chapter emphasizes the spiritual nature of humans and the importance of nurturing this aspect to develop a deep and effective relationship with God, particularly in the ministry of prayer.

Key Points

- Humans are created as spirits with the ability to see, hear, smell, hunger, thirst, walk, and speak spiritually.
- Being more aware of our spirit rather than our body or soul enhances our ability to interact with God.
- Spiritual people are sensitive to the unseen realm and can have varied spiritual experiences.
- Many cultures historically and presently engage deeply in spiritual practices and beliefs.
- Believers should focus on spiritual awareness and responsiveness to God, rather than just general spirituality.
- True prayer involves direct connection and co-laboring with God, aligning with His will.

Key Themes

- **Spiritual Capabilities:** Humans have innate spiritual abilities, such as spiritual sight and hearing, which enable interaction with God. Recognizing and nurturing these capabilities is essential for a fulfilling spiritual life.

- **Dominance of the Spirit:** To function as whole beings, our spirit should be the dominant part of our being. This dominance allows us to navigate life more effectively, guided by spiritual insights rather than just physical or emotional responses.
- **Global Spiritual Awareness:** Across cultures and histories, people have demonstrated deep spiritual awareness and practices. This universal spiritual inclination highlights the human spirit's intrinsic desire for connection with the divine.
- **Purposeful Spirituality:** The goal of spiritual awareness is not just to be spiritual, but to be consciously connected to God and to work together with Him. This focused spirituality ensures that our spiritual activities align with God's purposes.
- **Prayer as Co-Laboring:** True prayer is a privileged form of interaction with God, involving more than just a daily discipline. It is an opportunity to commune with God and participate in His divine work, representing His will on earth.

Conclusion

The chapter calls readers to recognize and embrace their spiritual nature, nurturing their spirit to develop a deeper relationship with God. By focusing on spiritual awareness and responsiveness to God, believers can transform their prayer life into a powerful partnership with the divine. This approach not only enriches their spiritual journey but also aligns their actions with God's purposes, leading to a more fulfilling and impactful life.

CHAPTER 6

HOUSE OF PRAYER

Bible Verse

"Then he returned to the disciples and found them asleep. He said to Peter, 'Couldn't you watch with me even one hour? Keep watch and pray, so that you will not give in to temptation. For the spirit is willing, but the body is weak!'" - Matthew 26:40-41 (NLT)

Introduction

This chapter discusses the concept of our bodies as temples of the Holy Spirit and emphasizes the importance of aligning our physical and spiritual selves to effectively participate in prayer. It explores the necessity of spiritual awareness and the discipline required to ensure our bodies facilitate rather than hinder our spiritual engagement.

Word of Wisdom

"Let's not see our bodies as the enemy but present them to God for His use."

Main Theme

The chapter highlights the significance of recognizing our bodies as houses of prayer, stressing the need to consecrate our physical selves for God's purposes and maintain a harmonious balance between body, soul, and spirit.

Key Points

- Audible instances of God's voice are rare but significant, such as Saul's encounter on the road to Damascus.
- Spiritual awareness involves hearing and seeing with our spiritual senses.
- Jesus emphasized the willingness of the spirit and the weakness of the body in prayer.
- Proper treatment and discipline of our bodies are essential for effective spiritual work.
- Our bodies are temples of the Holy Spirit and should be honored and consecrated for God's use.
- Spiritual and natural senses work together in prayer to fulfill God's purposes.

Key Themes

- **Spiritual and Physical Alignment:** Effective prayer requires the alignment of our spiritual and physical selves. This involves recognizing our bodies as instruments for God's purposes and ensuring they facilitate rather than hinder our spiritual activities.

- **Discipline and Prioritization:** Disciplining our bodies and maintaining their proper priority is crucial for effective spiritual work. The chapter emphasizes the importance of controlling our bodies rather than letting them control our spiritual pursuits.
- **Temple of the Holy Spirit:** Our bodies, as temples of the Holy Spirit, are sacred and should be consecrated for holy use. This understanding encourages believers to treat their bodies with respect and use them for God's glory.
- **Role of Worship and Prayer:** Worship and prayer are key practices that help maintain the balance between body and spirit. Presenting our bodies to God in worship consecrates them for His use and enhances our spiritual awareness.
- **Watching in Prayer:** The concept of watching in prayer involves being spiritually vigilant and responsive to God's guidance. This practice requires both spiritual and natural senses to discern God's will and report it through prayer.

Conclusion

The chapter calls readers to embrace the understanding of their bodies as houses of prayer, encouraging them to consecrate their physical selves for God's purposes. By maintaining discipline and prioritizing their spiritual awareness, believers can effectively participate in prayer and fulfill God's will. This harmonious balance between body, soul, and spirit transforms their prayer life and enhances their spiritual journey.

CHAPTER 7

COME TO MOUNT ZION

Bible Verse

"No, you have come to Mount Zion, to the city of the living God, the heavenly Jerusalem, and to countless thousands of angels in a joyful gathering." - Hebrews 12:22 (NLT)

Introduction

This chapter explores the spiritual significance of Mount Zion, contrasting it with Mount Sinai. It emphasizes the spiritual reality believers enter into when they interact with God and the various beings that inhabit this divine realm.

Word of Wisdom

"What a priceless privilege it is to pray and represent this new covenant ratified by Jesus' own blood."

Main Theme

The chapter underscores the importance of understanding and engaging with the spiritual realm of Mount Zion, where believers work with God and encounter various spiritual beings in the presence of God.

Key Points

• Mount Sinai represents the Old Testament experience, characterized by physical manifestations and fear.

• Mount Zion, the heavenly Jerusalem, is where believers now come to interact with God.

• In Mount Zion, believers encounter countless angels in joyful gathering.

• The assembly of God's firstborn children includes all believers, both on earth and in heaven.

• God Himself is the judge over all things, aligning believers' prayers with His will.

• The sprinkled blood of Jesus speaks of forgiveness and redemption, unlike the blood of Abel.

Key Themes

• **Contrast Between Mount Sinai and Mount Zion:** Mount Sinai is associated with fear and physical manifestations, while Mount Zion represents a spiritual realm where believers interact with God.

This contrast helps believers understand their current spiritual position and the nature of their interactions with God.

- **Angels in Joyful Gathering:** The presence of countless angels in Mount Zion highlights their role in God's purposes. These angels assist believers in understanding God's plans, providing protection, and delivering messages, all while living in constant joy in God's presence.

- **Assembly of God's Firstborn Children:** This assembly includes all believers, emphasizing the unity and continuity of the Body of Christ. Whether in heaven or on earth, believers are part of this divine assembly, working together in God's purposes.

- **God as the Righteous Judge:** Coming to God, the righteous judge, ensures that believers' prayers and actions are aligned with His will. This alignment is crucial for effective spiritual work and maintaining true spiritual pitch.

- **The Power of Jesus' Blood:** The sprinkled blood of Jesus in Mount Zion speaks of forgiveness and redemption. Understanding the power of this blood is essential for believers as they work with God, offering a correct way to speak and dispense God's mercy and love.

Conclusion

The chapter calls readers to embrace their spiritual position in Mount Zion, understanding the significance of this divine realm and the beings that inhabit it. By engaging with God and aligning their prayers with His will, believers can effectively participate in His purposes. The emphasis on the sprinkled blood of Jesus as a source of forgiveness and redemption underscores the privilege and responsibility of working with God in this spiritual realm.

❧

CHAPTER 8

THE GATE

Bible Verse

"Yes, I am the gate. Those who come in through me will be saved. They will come and go freely and will find good pastures." - John 10:9 (NLT)

Introduction

T his chapter emphasizes the importance of accessing the spiritual realm through Jesus, the Gate. It highlights the various ways people attempt to enter the spiritual realm and stresses the necessity of using the legitimate, God-provided way to ensure effective and safe spiritual interactions.

Word of Wisdom

"From that place of independence it is easy to slip into working for God rather than the privilege of working with Him."

Main Theme

The chapter underscores the importance of entering the spiritual realm through Jesus, ensuring that our spiritual activities are aligned with God's will and guided by His presence.

Key Points

• Different rooms in a home serve specific functions, just as there are specific ways to enter the spiritual realm.

• Unauthorized means of accessing the spiritual realm are likened to thieves and robbers.

• Jesus, as the Gate, provides legitimate access to the spiritual realm.

• The Holy Spirit guides us to Jesus, highlighting His titles and functions.

• Accessing the spiritual realm through Jesus ensures safety and alignment with God's will.

• Dependence on Jesus is essential for true spiritual activity and avoiding independent spiritual works.

Key Themes

• **Jesus as the Gate:** Jesus identifies Himself as the Gate, the legitimate way to access the spiritual realm. This title not only highlights His role but also emphasizes the importance of entering through Him for safe and effective spiritual interaction.

- **Unauthorized Access:** Many cultures and practices seek to enter the spiritual realm through unauthorized means, such as horoscopes and drugs. These methods are contrasted with the proper access through Jesus, emphasizing the importance of using the right entrance.
- **Holy Spirit's Guidance:** The Holy Spirit plays a crucial role in guiding believers to Jesus, helping them recognize His titles and functions. This guidance ensures that believers enter the spiritual realm through the correct means and remain aligned with God's purposes.
- **Dependence on Jesus:** The chapter stresses the necessity of continual dependence on Jesus for all spiritual activities. Independent spiritual works are cautioned against, as they can lead to misalignment with God's will and potential spiritual dangers.
- **Experiences Beyond the Gate:** Entering the spiritual realm through Jesus opens up endless and wonderful possibilities. Believers can receive direction, reassurance, and knowledge, all guided by Jesus' presence and influence.

Conclusion

The chapter calls readers to recognize and embrace Jesus as the Gate to the spiritual realm. By relying on the Holy Spirit's guidance and maintaining a dependent relationship with Jesus, believers can safely and effectively engage in spiritual activities.

This approach ensures that their spiritual experiences are aligned with God's will and contribute to a deeper, more fulfilling relationship with Him.

❧

CHAPTER 9

THE STAIRWAY

Bible Verse

"Then he [Jesus] said, 'I tell you the truth, you will all see heaven open and the angels of God going up and down on the Son of Man, the One Who is the stairway between heaven and earth.'" - John 1:51 (NLT)

Introduction

This chapter explores the concept of a spiritual stairway between heaven and earth, introduced through Jacob's dream and fulfilled in Jesus. It emphasizes that Jesus is the access point to the spiritual realm, allowing believers to ascend and gain spiritual visibility and awareness.

Word of Wisdom

"Let's not wait until we are perfect but trust His perfection on our behalf."

Main Theme

The chapter highlights Jesus as the spiritual stairway, the essential means for believers to access the supernatural realm, grow in spiritual awareness, and fulfill God's purposes despite human imperfections.

Key Points

• Jacob's dream of a stairway to heaven illustrates a connection between the seen and unseen worlds.

• Despite human flaws, God's plans and purposes are fulfilled through obedience and humility.

• Jesus identifies Himself as the stairway, the true means of spiritual access.

• Ascending the stairway provides increasing spiritual visibility and awareness.

• Biblical examples like John and Paul demonstrate the full ascent into spiritual realms.

• Jesus, as the stairway, is the only way to access and interact with the spiritual realm.

Key Themes

• **Jesus as the Spiritual Stairway:** Jesus is the connection between earth and heaven, enabling believers to ascend spiritually. This role is not just symbolic but functional, providing a means to access the supernatural realm.

- **God's Plans Amid Human Imperfection:** The story of Jacob shows that God's purposes prevail despite human flaws and deceptions. Trusting in God's perfection and being responsive to His will are key to fulfilling His plans.
- **Increasing Spiritual Awareness:** Ascending the spiritual stairway through Jesus leads to greater spiritual visibility and understanding. Each step provides clearer insights and deeper awareness of spiritual realities.
- **Biblical Examples of Spiritual Ascent:** John and Paul exemplify complete spiritual ascent, reaching high levels of spiritual awareness and clarity. Their experiences highlight the possibilities available to believers who fully embrace Jesus as their access point.
- **Exclusive Access Through Jesus:** Emphasizing Jesus as the sole means of entering the spiritual realm ensures that believers remain aligned with God's will. This exclusive access safeguards against unauthorized and potentially harmful spiritual practices.

Conclusion

The chapter calls readers to recognize and embrace Jesus as the spiritual stairway, the essential means for accessing the supernatural realm. By ascending through Jesus, believers can gain greater spiritual visibility, fulfill God's purposes, and navigate the spiritual realm with clarity and confidence. This approach reinforces the importance of depending solely on Jesus for spiritual growth and interaction.

❦

CHAPTER 10

THE LIVING AND WRITTEN WORD

Bible Verse

"In the beginning the Word already existed. The Word was with God, and the Word was God." - John 1:1 (NLT)

Introduction

This chapter emphasizes the importance of both the living and written Word of God as steps on the spiritual stairway, providing access to God and the spirit realm. It highlights how the Word of God serves as a critical guide to understand His will and avoid deception by the devil.

Word of Wisdom

"Let's not wait until we are perfect but trust His perfection on our behalf."

Main Theme

The chapter underscores the significance of the written and living Word of God in providing access to the spiritual realm, offering clarity, guidance, and alignment with God's will.

Key Points

• God's Word is a perfect expression of Himself and a means to access the spiritual realm.

• The written Word reveals God's will and the Living Word, Jesus.

• Misinterpretation of scripture can lead to error, highlighting the need for alignment with Jesus' teachings.

• The Holy Spirit guides believers in understanding and applying the Word.

• Four areas of the written Word useful in prayer are promises, scriptural prayers, praise, and prophecy.

• Using God's promises helps believers escape natural realm limitations and align with His will.

Key Themes

• **The Word as a Spiritual Stairway:**
  Both the written and living Word of God act as steps on a spiritual stairway, providing access to God and the spirit realm. This metaphor emphasizes the

Word's role in guiding believers to spiritual insights and experiences.

- **Role of the Written Word:** The written Word of God is crucial for determining His will, providing clarity and preventing deception. It serves as a reliable source of truth that aligns believers with God's purposes.

- **Jesus as the Living Word:** Jesus, the Living Word, is central to understanding and interpreting the written Word. His life and teachings provide the perfect example of how to live according to God's will.

- **Holy Spirit's Guidance:** The Holy Spirit plays a vital role in helping believers understand and apply the Word of God. This divine guidance ensures that believers correctly interpret scripture and use it effectively in their spiritual lives.

- **Four Areas of the Word in Prayer:** Promises, scriptural prayers, praise, and prophecy are four key areas of the Word that the Holy Spirit directs believers to in prayer. These elements provide access to the spirit realm and facilitate alignment with God's will.

Conclusion

The chapter encourages readers to deeply engage with both the written and living Word of God, allowing it to guide their spiritual journey and prayer life. By relying on the Holy Spirit's guidance and embracing the truths revealed in scripture, believers can access the spiritual realm, gain divine insights, and align their lives with God's will. This approach ensures a balanced and effective spiritual life, rooted in the unchanging truth of God's Word.

❧

CHAPTER 11

PRAYER AND PRAISE

Bible Verse

"Rejoice always, pray without ceasing, in everything give thanks; for this is the will of God in Christ Jesus for you."
- 1 Thessalonians 5:16-18 (NKJV)

Introduction

This chapter delves into the power of prayer and praise as access points to the spiritual realm, continuing from the previous discussion on promises. It highlights the transformative effect of praying scriptural prayers and engaging in heartfelt praise to elevate our spiritual awareness and align with God's presence.

Word of Wisdom

"Pray until your eyes are actually looking at the One you're talking to."

Main Theme

The chapter emphasizes the significance of using prayer and praise to shift from natural concerns to spiritual realities, allowing believers to access God's presence, gain divine insight, and experience transformative outcomes.

Key Points

• Paul's prayers in the Epistles are powerful tools for accessing the spirit realm.

• Praying these Holy Spirit-inspired prayers can shift our perspective from the natural to the spiritual.

• Praise changes our focus from problems to God, facilitating spiritual ascendancy.

• True prayer involves moving beyond worry and fear to genuine communion with God.

• Examples from the Bible, such as Paul and Silas, demonstrate the power of praise in dire situations.

• Once in the spirit, additional scriptures and insights often come to mind, providing further clarity and direction.

Key Themes

• **Paul's Scriptural Prayers:** The prayers recorded in Paul's epistles are inspired by the Holy Spirit and provide powerful access to the spiritual realm. By praying these prayers in faith, believers can experience a shift into a deeper spiritual awareness and understanding.

- **Transformative Power of Praise:** Praise is a vital tool for changing our focus from natural problems to God's greatness. It enables believers to ascend into the spirit, where they can see things from God's perspective and experience His power and presence.
- **Examples of Praise in Adversity:** The stories of 2 Chronicles 20 and Acts 16 illustrate how praise can lead to miraculous outcomes. These examples show that even in the most challenging circumstances, praising God can bring about divine intervention and victory.
- **Importance of Spiritual Focus in Prayer:** Genuine prayer involves looking beyond the natural realm and entering into God's presence. This spiritual focus ensures that our prayers are aligned with God's will and filled with faith rather than fear.
- **Ongoing Revelation in the Spirit:** Once believers enter the spirit through prayer and praise, they often receive additional scriptures and insights. This ongoing revelation provides further guidance and clarity, enhancing their prayer life and spiritual effectiveness.

Conclusion

The chapter encourages readers to incorporate Paul's scriptural prayers and heartfelt praise into their spiritual practices. By doing so, they can shift from a natural to a spiritual focus, access God's presence, and receive divine insights and solutions. This approach transforms their prayer life, making it more powerful and aligned with God's will.

❧❦❧

CHAPTER 12

PROPHECIES

Bible Verse

"This charge and admonition I commit in trust to you, Timothy, my son, in accordance with prophetic intimations which I formerly received concerning you, so that inspired and aided by them you may wage the good warfare." - 1 Timothy 1:18 (AMPC)

Introduction

This chapter explores how prophecies serve as access points to the spiritual realm, enabling believers to move beyond their natural circumstances into the divine perspective. Using Daniel's experience with Jeremiah's prophecy as a primary example, it emphasizes the power of prophecies in guiding prayer and aligning with God's will.

Word of Wisdom

"Prophecy becomes an access for you

to get into the spirit where there could be more to be said, more to be seen, more to be declared or prayed."

Main Theme

The chapter highlights the importance of prophecies in providing spiritual access, facilitating divine understanding, and enabling believers to participate in God's purposes through prayer and declaration.

Key Points

• Daniel's prayer was inspired by Jeremiah's prophecy about the end of Israel's captivity.

• Prophecies can shift our focus from natural circumstances to God's perspective.

• The spirit realm offers timeless insights, clarifying God's purposes and plans.

• Acknowledging past prophecies can unlock further revelation and understanding.

• Prophecies can be used to wage spiritual warfare effectively.

• Personal and corporate prophecies guide and encourage believers in fulfilling God's will.

Key Themes

• **Daniel's Use of Prophecy in Prayer:** Daniel's discovery of Jeremiah's prophecy led him to pray for Israel's restoration, shifting his focus from his physical location in Babylon to God's divine plan. This example shows how prophecies can inspire prayer and provide spiritual access.

- **Spiritual Awareness Through Prophecy:** Prophecies elevate believers' spiritual awareness, allowing them to see God's purposes and plans. This heightened awareness enables them to participate in divine activities and gain clarity on future events.

- **Importance of Recognizing Past Prophecies:** Acknowledging and valuing previous prophecies is crucial for receiving further revelation. This practice helps believers connect with the spirit of prophecy and gain deeper insights into God's plans.

- **Prophecies as Tools for Spiritual Warfare:** Prophecies are not just for inspiration but are practical tools for waging spiritual warfare. Believers can use prophetic words to transition from the natural to the spiritual realm, where they can see and declare God's will.

- **Collective Participation in God's Purposes:** Prophecies enable believers to work together with others who have received similar revelations. This collective participation strengthens the Church's ability to fulfill God's purposes on earth.

Conclusion

The chapter calls readers to embrace prophecies as vital tools for accessing the spiritual realm and

aligning with God's will. By recognizing and valuing prophetic words, believers can gain divine insights, wage effective spiritual warfare, and participate collectively in God's purposes. This approach transforms their prayer life, making it more powerful and aligned with God's divine plan.

❦

CHAPTER 13

THE SPIRIT REALM

Bible Verse

"It was the Lord's Day, and I was worshiping in the Spirit." - Revelation 1:10 (NLT)

Introduction

This chapter explores the concept of the spirit realm, illustrating how believers can transcend physical limitations and engage with God's purposes through spiritual access. Using examples from personal experiences and biblical narratives, it emphasizes the power of being in the spirit, regardless of physical location.

Word of Wisdom

"You are never, ever bound to your physical location or to any other elements of your environment if you know how to get in the spirit."

Main Theme

The chapter highlights the importance of accessing the spirit realm to work with God, showing that physical restrictions do not limit spiritual engagement and influence.

Key Points

• John was exiled on Patmos but continued to have significant spiritual influence.

• Being in the spirit transcends physical and environmental limitations.

• Offense, self-pity, and natural focus can hinder spiritual effectiveness.

• The spirit realm offers clarity and insight into God's purposes.

• Believers can spiritually travel and impact various locations through prayer.

• The devil tries to keep believers in the flesh to hinder their spiritual potential.

Key Themes

• **Transcending Physical Limitations:**
John's exile on Patmos serves as a powerful example of how physical location does not limit spiritual influence. By being in the spirit, John received and documented the Revelation, impacting the Church for generations.

- **Avoiding Fleshly Distractions:**
  Offense, self-pity, and natural distractions
  can confine believers to the flesh,
  hindering their spiritual effectiveness.
  Staying God-conscious and avoiding these
  pitfalls is crucial for spiritual engagement.
- **Power of Spiritual Awareness:** When
  believers are in the spirit, they are most
  aware of God, His Word, and the realities
  of the spirit realm. This awareness enables
  them to cooperate with God effectively
  and understand their divine potential.
- **Impacting the World Through
  Prayer:** Despite physical restrictions,
  believers can spiritually travel and impact
  various regions through prayer. The
  author's experience during COVID-19
  lockdowns illustrates this principle.
- **Living in the Spirit:** The spirit realm is
  not a distant place but accessible through
  faith. Believers can purposefully enter and
  operate in the spirit, using their spiritual
  senses to work with God.

Conclusion

The chapter encourages readers to embrace the
spirit realm as their true place of influence and effectiveness. By avoiding fleshly distractions and
staying spiritually aware, believers can transcend
physical limitations and work with God to impact
the world. This approach transforms their prayer
life, making it more powerful and aligned with
God's purposes.

CHAPTER 14

SEEING AND HEARING IN THE SPIRIT

Bible Verse

"It was the Lord's Day, and I was worshiping in the Spirit. Suddenly, I heard behind me a loud voice like a trumpet blast." - Revelation 1:10 (NLT)

Introduction

This chapter delves into the concept of seeing and hearing in the spirit, using the apostle John's experience on the island of Patmos as a primary example. It emphasizes the importance of spiritual awareness and how it enables believers to receive divine direction and revelation.

Word of Wisdom

"Prayer is not the place where you try to change a circumstance, your relatives, your nation, and the world. That kind of

*thinking puts the responsibility of being
God on your shoulders."*

Main Theme

The chapter focuses on the significance of spiritual
perception, highlighting how believers can hear and
see in the spirit to receive guidance and revelation
from God.

Key Points

• John's spiritual ears and eyes allowed him to hear
and see divine revelations.

• Spiritual awareness disconnects us from the overwhelming voices of the natural world.

• Fixating on natural circumstances can hinder spiritual effectiveness.

• Being in the spirit provides a clear perspective
aligned with God's will.

• Effective Kingdom work requires engagement in
the spirit.

• Prayer shifts focus from the problem to God and
His Word.

Key Themes

• **John's Spiritual Perception:** John's
experience on Patmos illustrates the power
of spiritual perception. He heard and saw

divine revelations, emphasizing that spiritual senses can perceive beyond the natural realm.

- **Disconnecting from Natural Voices:** To be effective in prayer, believers must disconnect from the overwhelming voices of the natural world. John's focus on spiritual realities rather than his physical circumstances exemplifies this principle.
- **Fixation on Natural Circumstances:** Fixating on natural circumstances and voices leads to fear, anger, and despair. Believers are encouraged to shift their focus to God and His Word to maintain spiritual effectiveness.
- **Engagement in the Spirit:** Kingdom work requires engagement in the spirit. John's revelations came from being in the spirit, showing that effective prayer and divine direction are accessed through spiritual engagement.
- **Prayer as Shifting Focus:** Prayer is not about trying to change circumstances directly but about shifting focus from problems to God. Effective prayer involves becoming aware of the Lord and receiving His guidance.

Conclusion

The chapter encourages readers to develop their spiritual perception by focusing on God and His Word rather than natural circumstances. By engaging in the spirit, believers can receive divine guidance and work effectively with God. The responsibility is not to be God but to partner with Him in prayer, trusting Him to accomplish His will.

తింత

CHAPTER 15

PROPHETIC PRAYER

Bible Verse

"If you love me, obey my commandments." - John 14:15 (NLT)

Introduction

This chapter explores the concept of prophetic prayer, emphasizing how believers can participate in bringing God's purposes to pass on Earth through Spirit-led, inspired prayer. It highlights the importance of discerning and declaring God's plans as revealed through prophecy.

Word of Wisdom

"Prayer is not the place where you try to change a circumstance, your relatives, your nation, and the world. That kind of thinking puts the responsibility of being God on your shoulders."

Main Theme

Prophetic prayer involves praying inspired by the Holy Spirit, aligning with God's will, and speaking forth His purposes. It is a form of prayer that relies on divine revelation rather than natural understanding.

Key Points

• Prophetic prayer is inspired by the Holy Spirit, not driven by natural senses.

• Believers can help fulfill God's purposes on Earth through prophetic prayer.

• The term "prophesy" in 1 Corinthians 14 refers primarily to forthtelling God's mind and message.

• Prophetic prayer is spontaneous and Spirit-led, not rehearsed or memorized.

• Using God's Word in prayer aligns believers with His will and invites further divine guidance.

• Spirit-led prayer assemblies are powerful, unrehearsed, and directed by the Holy Spirit.

Key Themes

• **Prophetic Prayer Defined:** Prophetic prayer is inspired by divine revelation, allowing believers to see and understand God's plans and declare them in prayer. It involves discerning God's will and speaking it forth under the guidance of the Holy Spirit.

- **Role of the Holy Spirit:** The Holy Spirit plays a crucial role in guiding prophetic prayer. By directing believers to specific scriptures, promises, and prophecies, the Holy Spirit helps them align their prayers with God's purposes and stay on track.
- **Individual and Corporate Prayer:** While individual prophetic prayer is important, praying in a group or congregation led by the Holy Spirit can be incredibly powerful. This collective prayer, directed by the spirit of prophecy, creates a unified and potent force in the spiritual realm.
- **Learning to Follow the Spirit:** Believers are encouraged to develop their personal relationship with Jesus and learn to follow the Holy Spirit's leading in their prayer life. Imitating others can lead to spiritual misdirection; personal spiritual growth requires recognizing the Holy Spirit's unique guidance.
- **Impact of Prophetic Prayer:** Prophetic prayer can lead to significant, tangible outcomes, sometimes revealed later. The story of the taxi driver who was saved after being prayed for is an example of how Spirit-led prayer can have life-changing effects, demonstrating God's orchestration in prayer.

Conclusion

Prophetic prayer allows believers to partner with God in fulfilling His divine purposes on Earth. By being attuned to the Holy Spirit and using God's Word as a foundation, believers can pray effectively and bring about God's will. This cooperation with the divine is both a privilege and a responsibility, leading to profound spiritual growth and impactful prayer.

❧

CHAPTER 16

TENDER COMPASSION

Bible Verse

*"But you, O Lord, are a God of compassion and mercy,
slow to get angry and filled with unfailing love and
faithfulness." - Psalm 86:15 (NLT)*

Introduction

In this chapter, the focus is on understanding and cooperating with God's compassion. It emphasizes the importance of tender compassion in our walk with God, highlighting how His perfect love makes Him tender toward everyone.

Word of Wisdom

"Compassion becomes a bridge between the hurting person and God, who is willing and able to help them."

Main Theme

Compassion is a fundamental aspect of God's love, moving Him and should move us to action, especially toward those who are hurting. Understanding and responding to this compassion is crucial for effective ministry and representation of God's love.

Key Points

• Compassion is an aspect of God's love, making Him tender towards everyone.

• Jesus' ministry was often driven by His compassion for people.

• Tenderness indicates God's perfect love and sensitivity to people's pain.

• Responding to compassion means moving towards and helping those who are hurting.

• Compassion bridges the gap between hurting people and God's healing power.

• True ministry involves holding onto both God and the hurting with compassion.

Key Themes

- **God's Compassion:** God is full of compassion and never shows irritation or disgust toward anyone. His tender love moves Him toward people, and this is reflected in how He responds to their needs.

- **Jesus' Compassion in Action:** Jesus' ministry was frequently motivated by compassion. His miracles, healings, and teachings were all driven by His tender love and sensitivity to people's suffering.
- **Compassion and Tenderness:** Tenderness is a significant aspect of compassion, making one acutely sensitive to others' pain. This sensitivity is not about personal greatness but about reflecting God's perfect love.
- **Compassion in Ministry:** Effective ministry requires responding to God's compassion. This involves a willingness to feel others' pain and take action to help them, rather than turning away or merely sympathizing.
- **The Bridge of Compassion:** Compassionate ministry is like a bridge, holding onto the hurting person with one hand and God with the other. This connection allows God's healing and deliverance to flow through us to those in need.

Conclusion

Compassion is a powerful and essential part of working with God. By holding onto both God and the hurting with tender compassion, believers can become channels of His love, healing, and deliverance. True ministry is not just about being spiritual but about being moved by God's compassion to help those in need.

CHAPTER 17

THE ROCK

Bible Verse

"Trust in the Lord always, for the Lord God is the eternal Rock." - Isaiah 26:4 (NLT)

Introduction

This chapter explores the aspect of Jesus as the Rock, emphasizing His unchanging and eternal nature. The author draws parallels between the enduring strength of physical rock formations and the steadfastness of God, highlighting the importance of relying on Him for stability and truth.

Word of Wisdom

"Truth, real truth, can only be found in the One who said, 'I am the truth.'"

Main Theme

Understanding Jesus as the Rock of Ages provides believers with a foundation of stability, eternal truth, and unwavering faith, helping them navigate life's uncertainties and spiritual battles.

Key Points

• The Rock symbolizes God's eternal and unchanging nature.

• Jesus is described as the Alpha and Omega, emphasizing His eternal existence.

• Trusting in God provides access to eternal truths about the past, present, and future.

• The devil's lies can only be countered by the eternal truth found in Jesus.

• True faith begins and ends with Jesus, the Author and Finisher of our faith.

• God's promises and prophecies reveal the end from the beginning, providing assurance of His plans.

Key Themes

• **God's Eternal Nature:** God is described as the Rock of Ages, emphasizing His unchanging and everlasting nature. This eternal characteristic assures believers that God's truths and promises are reliable and enduring.

- **Access to Eternal Truth:** In the spirit, believers can access eternal truths about the past, present, and future. This divine perspective helps them understand God's plans and counters the devil's lies.
- **Jesus as the Author and Finisher:** Jesus is both the beginning and the end of our faith. This concept is illustrated by a circle, where the starting point and the endpoint are the same, highlighting the closeness and certainty of God's plans.
- **Stability in God's Promises:** Just as rock formations remain unchanged over time, God's promises and prophecies are steadfast. They reveal how things will end, providing believers with confidence and assurance in God's ultimate plan.
- **Danger of Seeking Truth Outside God:** The chapter warns against seeking knowledge through horoscopes, tarot cards, and other occult practices. True knowledge and freedom come only from God, who is the ultimate source of truth.

Conclusion

Understanding and relying on Jesus as the Rock provides believers with a solid foundation of faith and truth. By trusting in God's eternal nature and promises, they can navigate life's challenges with confidence and assurance, knowing that the end is secure in Him.

CHAPTER 18

THE REST

Bible Verse

"So there is a special rest still waiting for the people of God." - Hebrews 4:9 (NLT)

Introduction

This chapter delves into the concept of rest that comes from God, contrasting it with ordinary methods of relaxation. Using the Old Testament story of Moses sitting on a stone during battle, the chapter illustrates how true rest, rooted in God's eternal nature, provides unparalleled support and victory.

Word of Wisdom

"In this place of rest in the spirit, prayer shifts from trying to get God to do something to the delight of discovering what He has already willed!"

Main Theme

The chapter emphasizes the importance of entering God's rest, a spiritual state that provides peace, support, and clarity, enabling believers to work effectively with God and witness His purposes being fulfilled.

Key Points

• True rest comes from God and is not limited to physical relaxation.

• Moses' victory over Amalek illustrates the power of resting on the Rock.

• God's rest allows believers to become one with His will and purposes.

• Entering God's rest involves a shift from striving to trusting in His completed works.

• The spirit realm, where rest is found, transcends time and space, offering eternal perspective.

• Believers are encouraged to labor to enter this rest, ceasing from their own efforts.

Key Themes

• **Divine Rest and Support:** The story of Moses sitting on a stone during battle highlights how resting on the Rock (God) provides support and victory. This divine rest surpasses physical relaxation, enabling believers to accomplish God's purposes.

- **Eternal Perspective:** Being in the spirit and entering God's rest allows believers to transcend the confines of time and space. This eternal perspective provides clarity and assurance, revealing God's truths about the past, present, and future.
- **Faith and Obedience:** Entering God's rest requires faith and obedience. Doubt and disobedience hinder access to this rest, while belief and trust in God enable believers to experience His promises and peace.
- **Shift from Striving to Trusting:** In God's rest, believers move from striving to achieve outcomes to trusting in God's completed works. This shift transforms prayer into a joyful discovery of God's already established plans.
- **Encouragement to Enter Rest:** Believers are encouraged to labor to enter God's rest, supporting one another in this journey. Entering rest involves ceasing from personal efforts and aligning with God's eternal purposes.

Conclusion

Entering God's rest is essential for effective prayer and working with Him. This rest, rooted in God's eternal nature, offers unparalleled support, clarity, and peace. Believers are called to trust in God's completed works and discover the delight of His already established plans.

❧❦❧

CHAPTER 19

THE LABOR

Bible Verse

"Let us labor therefore to enter into that rest, lest any man fall after the same example of unbelief." - Hebrews 4:11 (KJV)

Introduction

T his chapter explores the concept of laboring to enter God's rest. Through the example of Jesus facing the cross with unwavering hope and faith, it illustrates how believers can achieve a divine rest that transcends physical relaxation. This rest is essential for effective prayer and working with God.

Word of Wisdom

"Labor to get into rest because it is in 'rest' that you discover what God has

already determined and your prayer from that point is in faith."

Main Theme

The chapter emphasizes the necessity of laboring to enter God's rest, a spiritual state where believers can discover God's already established will and work with Him in faith and confidence.

Key Points

• True rest is a spiritual state, not just physical relaxation.

• Jesus faced the cross with rest in His heart, knowing God's plan.

• Believers must come to Jesus to receive rest.

• Laboring to enter rest involves shifting focus from the natural to the spiritual realm.

• God's work is accomplished through His power, not human effort.

• Prayer from a place of rest is effective and aligned with God's will.

Key Themes

- **Jesus' Example of Rest:** Jesus faced the cross with unwavering confidence, knowing God's plan. His rest came from a deep awareness of His Father's presence, which allowed Him to endure torture and death with hope.
- **Invitation to Rest:** Jesus invites the weary to come to Him for rest. This rest is not just physical but a profound spiritual refreshing that relieves the soul and aligns believers with God's will.
- **Laboring to Enter Rest:** Believers must labor to enter God's rest, which involves shifting focus from natural circumstances to the spiritual realm where God's will is already established. This labor is essential for discovering and cooperating with God's purposes.
- **Rest in the Spirit:** True prayer happens in the spirit, where believers are free from the clamor of the natural world. Being in the spirit allows them to be more aware of God and His plans, leading to effective and faith-filled prayers.
- **God's Completed Works:** God's plans and purposes are already completed in the spiritual realm. Believers' labor in prayer should focus on discovering these completed works and aligning with them, rather than trying to achieve outcomes through human effort.

Conclusion

Entering God's rest is essential for effective prayer

and working with Him. This rest, rooted in faith and awareness of God's completed works, allows believers to pray and act from a place of confidence and alignment with His will. By laboring to enter this, believers can become powerful conduits of God's purposes on earth.

❦

CHAPTER 20

DRINKING FROM THE RIVER

Bible Verse

"Anyone who believes in me may come and drink! For the Scriptures declare, 'Rivers of living water will flow from his heart.'" - John 7:38 NLT

Introduction

This chapter delves into the concept of drinking from the river of living water, representing the Holy Spirit, and how it empowers believers in their prayer life. Through stories in Exodus and Jesus' teachings, it illustrates how believers can draw strength, refreshment, and divine purpose from Christ, the Rock.

Word of Wisdom

"The way you drink water is through your mouth. The way you drink this divine water is through your mouth as well."

Main Theme

The chapter emphasizes the importance of drinking from the spiritual river of living water, symbolizing the Holy Spirit, to access God's purposes and refreshment in prayer.

Key Points

• Jesus is the Rock that provides living water.

• Drinking from Jesus is drinking from the Holy Spirit.

• Praying in tongues allows believers to drink in God's purposes.

• Drinking from the Spirit refreshes and empowers believers.

• The Holy Spirit's water cleanses and purifies believers.

Key Themes

- **Jesus as the Rock:** In Exodus 17, Moses strikes the rock to provide water for the Israelites, symbolizing Jesus being struck for our sins. From Him flows life-giving water, representing the Holy Spirit, offering refreshment and sustenance.
- **Invitation to Drink:** Jesus invites anyone who is thirsty to come and drink from Him. This drinking refers to receiving the Holy Spirit, who flows from Jesus to believers, quenching their spiritual thirst and providing divine life.

- **Praying in the Spirit:** When believers pray in tongues, they drink from the river of living water. This practice allows them to access God's already established purposes and plans, bringing them into alignment with His will.
- **Refreshing and Cleansing:** The living water from Jesus purifies believers, removing spiritual contamination and distractions. It refreshes their souls, providing clarity and focus on God's higher thoughts and ways.
- **Overflowing Rivers:** As believers drink abundantly from Jesus, rivers of living water flow through them to others. This Spirit-fed prayer not only energizes them but also extends God's life and plans beyond their personal sphere.

Conclusion

Drinking from the river of living water is essential for spiritual refreshment and empowerment. By coming to Jesus and receiving the Holy Spirit, believers can access God's purposes and experience divine rest and clarity in their prayer life. Effortlessly, this divine life flows through them, impacting others and fulfilling God's plans on earth.

CHAPTER 21

THE PURPOSES OF GOD

Bible Verse

"For we are God's masterpiece. He has created us anew in Christ Jesus, so we can do the good things he planned for us long ago." - Ephesians 2:10 NLT

Introduction

This chapter explores the intentionality and purpose behind God's actions and plans, emphasizing that every individual is born with a specific purpose preordained by God. It illustrates how understanding and aligning with God's purposes can lead to a fulfilling and directed life.

Word of Wisdom

"Living a whole life with no plan or purpose is not fun. It's crazy!"

Main Theme

God has a purpose and plan for each person's life, established before they were born, and living according to this divine purpose brings fulfillment and alignment with God's will.

Key Points

• God's actions are intentional and based on His divine purpose.

• Jesus' life was purpose-driven, with His mission established before creation.

• Believers also have God-given purposes to fulfill.

• God's love for us remains unchanged regardless of our actions.

• Living in accordance with God's purpose brings delight to Him.

• Discovering God's purposes is invaluable and facilitated by the Holy Spirit.

Key Themes

- **Jesus' Purpose-Driven Life:** Jesus lived with a clear understanding of His purpose, fulfilling God's will through His teachings, miracles, and ultimately His sacrifice. His purpose was established before creation, and He consciously chose to fulfill it.
- **Believers' Divine Purpose:** Like Jesus, believers are born with specific purposes

planned by God. These purposes are our destiny, involving specific works that God prepared in advance for us to accomplish.

- **The Importance of Alignment with God's Will:** Aligning our lives with God's purposes brings pleasure to Him. It is not about earning His love, which is unconditional, but about living in a way that honors Him and produces good fruit.
- **Discovering and Fulfilling God's Purpose:** Discovering God's purpose for our lives involves seeking His will and being guided by the Holy Spirit. This discovery is more valuable than any earthly treasure and brings clarity and direction to our lives.
- **The Role of the Holy Spirit:** The Holy Spirit plays a crucial role in helping believers understand and fulfill God's purposes. He intercedes for us in harmony with God's will, ensuring that all things work together for our good and His plan.

Conclusion

Understanding and aligning with God's purposes for our lives leads to fulfillment and effective ministry. By seeking His will and being guided by the Holy Spirit, we can live purpose-driven lives that bring glory to God and accomplish His divine plans.

❦

CHAPTER 22

GEARS

Bible Verse

"For his Spirit searches out everything and shows us God's deep secrets." - 1 Corinthians 2:10 NLT

Introduction

This chapter uses the analogy of gears to illustrate how God's purposes and plans work together. Just as gears of different sizes and directions interlock to create movement, God's plans, with their intricate details, interact to fulfill His purposes. Understanding and engaging with these divine details through prayer is essential for believers.

Word of Wisdom

"There will be a collaboration of operations."

Main Theme

God's purposes and plans operate like interlocking gears, where each detail plays a crucial role. Believers are called to engage in prophetic prayer to understand and participate in these divine operations.

Key Points

• God's purposes are like gears, each with detailed plans that interlock to create movement.

• Details of God's plans are essential for the fulfillment of His purposes.

• Prophetic prayer helps reveal and understand these divine details.

• The Holy Spirit guides believers in praying and interpreting these mysteries.

• Interpretation of tongues can provide insight into God's plans and purposes.

Key Themes

- **Interlocking Purposes:** God's purposes, like gears, have intricate details that interlock and work together. Each purpose affects and activates others, demonstrating the interconnectedness of God's plans in both the kingdom of light and the kingdom of darkness.
- **Revealing God's Plans:** The Holy Spirit reveals the details of God's plans to believers. These plans are often hidden and

mysterious but are made known through
prayer and spiritual insight.

- **Prophetic Prayer:** Praying in tongues
  allows believers to speak mysteries and
  engage with God's plans. Interpretation of
  these prayers can provide clarity and
  understanding, helping believers align with
  God's will.

- **Examples of Divine Strategy:** The
  story of Joshua and the battle of Jericho
  illustrates how God provides detailed plans
  for victory. These plans are not human
  inventions but are divinely revealed and
  must be followed in faith.

- **Expecting Interpretation:** Believers
  should expect to receive interpretations of
  their prayers in tongues. These
  interpretations can come in various forms,
  such as immediate understanding, dreams,
  or through inspired teachings and
  prophecies from others.

Conclusion

Believers are invited to engage deeply with God's
plans through prayer, seeking and expecting to
understand the divine details. By positioning
themselves before God, they can receive insights
and participate in His purposes, much like gears
interlocking to create movement.

CHAPTER 23

DELIGHT IN THE DETAILS

Bible Verse

"But when the right time finally came, God sent his own Son." - Galatians 4:4 GNT

Introduction

This chapter explores the various detailed aspects of God's purposes. These details, revealed through prayer and the Holy Spirit, include the "What," "Who," "Where," "When," and "Wealth" of God's plans. By understanding and engaging with these details, believers can effectively participate in fulfilling divine purposes.

Word of Wisdom

"Delight in those details; each one holds so much value."

Main Theme

Understanding and engaging with the specific details of God's purposes allows believers to effectively participate in His divine plans.

Key Points

• God's purposes are intricate and detailed.

• Details include the "What," "Who," "Where," "When," and "Wealth" of His plans.

• Prophetic prayer reveals these details.

• Each detail contributes to the fulfillment of God's purposes.

• Believers are called to delight in and engage with these divine details.

Key Themes

- **What the Divine Purpose Is:** God's purposes are specific and intentional. For example, Jesus was sent as the Savior of the world, a purpose clearly stated in John 3:14-17. Understanding the "What" of God's plan helps in aligning prayer and actions with His will.
- **Who the People Are:** God's plans involve specific people, chosen to carry out His purposes. The roles of Mary, Joseph, the shepherds, and others in Jesus' birth illustrate how individuals are integral to divine plans. Believers may receive names

or roles through prophetic prayer, guiding them to pray for those destined to fulfill God's purposes.

- **Where the Place of God's Purpose Happens:** Specific locations are significant in God's plans. Jesus' birth in Bethlehem and His crucifixion in Jerusalem were divinely ordained places. Prayer can be focused on cities, regions, or countries that are pivotal to God's purposes, even if the reasons are not immediately clear.
- **When the Proper Time Is:** God's timing is precise. Jesus was born at the perfect time according to God's plan. Believers may feel an urgency in prayer as the time for a purpose's fulfillment approaches, similar to the increasing intensity before childbirth. Recognizing and praying for the timing of God's purposes is crucial.
- **Wealth and Provision for God's Purposes:** God provides resources for His plans. The gifts from the wise men to Jesus' family illustrate divine provision. Believers can pray for God's wealth to be directed to those fulfilling His purposes, ensuring that resources are available for His plans to be carried out.

Conclusion

Understanding the details of God's purposes allows believers to engage effectively in His plans. By delighting in these details and following the Holy Spirit's guidance, believers can play a significant role in the manifestation of God's will on earth. Each detail, whether it be the "What," "Who," "Where," "When," or "Wealth," holds immense value and contributes to the fulfillment of divine purposes.

❦

CHAPTER 24

PREPARING THE WAY OF THE LORD

Bible Verse

"Listen! It's the voice of someone shouting, 'Clear the way through the wilderness for the Lord! Make a straight highway through the wasteland for our God! Fill in the valleys, and level the mountains and hills. Straighten the curves, and smooth out the rough places. Then the glory of the Lord will be revealed, and all people will see it together. The Lord has spoken!'" - Isaiah 40:3-5 NLT

Introduction

The chapter likens prayer assignments to road construction, emphasizing that preparing the way for the Lord's return is an ongoing process that involves many stages and participants. Just as building a highway takes time and effort, so does the spiritual work of prayer in preparing for Jesus' second coming.

Word of Wisdom

"The Holy Spirit directs prayer for all of those sub-purposes, and the answers to these prayers are all converging toward the greatest and primary purpose of God."

Main Theme

Preparing the way for the Lord involves continuous and collaborative efforts in prayer, likened to the detailed and phased process of highway construction.

Key Points

• Prayer assignments are ongoing, not completed in one session.

• The process of preparing the way of the Lord involves various stages.

• The Holy Spirit directs the work and assigns tasks to different individuals.

• Many members of the Body of Christ contribute to fulfilling God's plans.

• The ultimate purpose is the second coming of Jesus.

Key Themes

• **Ongoing Nature of Prayer Assignments:** Prayer assignments are not completed in one session but involve continuous effort, similar to the phases of highway construction. Each prayer builds upon the previous one, contributing to the overall goal.

- **Stages of Spiritual Construction:** Just as road construction requires filling valleys and leveling mountains, prayer involves addressing different spiritual needs and obstacles. The Holy Spirit guides believers to focus on specific areas in each prayer session.
- **Collaborative Effort in the Body of Christ:** Preparing the way for the Lord is a collective task involving many believers. Each person has a role, and together, they fulfill God's overarching plans, much like how multiple workers contribute to a construction project.
- **John the Baptist's Role and Our Role:** John the Baptist prepared the way for Jesus' first coming. Now, the collective Body of Christ prepares for His return. Each believer's prayers and actions help pave the way for the Lord's second coming.
- **Pillars Supporting the Second Coming:** The overarching goal of Jesus' return is supported by various sub-purposes, represented as pillars. These sub-purposes, upheld by prayer, contribute to the ultimate fulfillment of God's primary plan.

Conclusion

Preparing the way for the Lord's return is a noble calling that involves ongoing, collaborative prayer efforts. Each prayer and action, guided by the Holy Spirit, contributes to the grand purpose of Jesus' second coming. By understanding and embracing our roles in this divine construction, we participate in God's magnificent plan.

৩৯৩

CHAPTER 25

THE JEWS, THE NATIONS, AND THE CHURCH

❧

Bible Verse

"Don't give offense to Jews or Gentiles or the church of God." - 1 Corinthians 10:32

Introduction

This chapter explores the diverse assignments within the body of Christ, emphasizing the unique and specific functions of each member. By identifying three primary groups—the Jews, the Nations, and the Church—the chapter highlights how these assignments relate to the broader Kingdom purposes.

Word of Wisdom

"If everyone is personally responsive to the Lord, the work of God will thrive and all the purposes of God will take place."

Main Theme

Understanding and responding to specific prayer assignments for the Jews, the Nations, and the Church as part of fulfilling God's Kingdom purposes.

Key Points

• Each part of the body of Christ has a unique and specific function.

• There are three primary groups identified for prayer: Jews, Gentiles, and the Church.

• Prayer assignments should be followed faithfully, akin to military assignments.

• General instructions to pray for all people are given in the Bible.

• Diversity in assignments should be respected and supported

Key Themes

- **Unique Functions in the Body:** Every organ and element in the body has a distinct role, contributing to the overall health and function. Similarly, every member of the body of Christ has a specific function and should focus on fulfilling their unique role.
- **Three Categories of People:** The Bible identifies three groups—Jews, Gentiles, and the Church. These categories guide prayer assignments, helping believers focus

on specific groups for intercession and ministry.

- **Prayer for the Jews:** There are individuals assigned to faithfully pray for the Jewish people and the nation of Israel, responding to a sense of urgency and following biblical precedent.
- **Prayer for the Nations:** Kingdom assignments often involve praying for specific nations, regions, or ethnic groups. Each demographic within the nations has unique needs and calls for dedicated prayer.
- **Prayer for the Church:** The Church, as a category, requires continual prayer. Paul's letters to the churches emphasize praying without ceasing for the believers, supporting their growth and mission.

Conclusion

Understanding and responding to specific prayer assignments for the Jews, the Nations, and the Church are vital to fulfilling God's purposes. Each believer's unique role contributes to the overall mission of the Kingdom. By embracing and faithfully executing these assignments, we ensure that the work of God thrives and His purposes are realized on earth.

CHAPTER 26

INDIVIDUALS

Bible Verse

*"Simon, Simon, Satan has asked to sift each of you like
wheat. But I have pleaded in prayer for you, Simon, that
your faith should not fail. So when you have repented and
turned to me again, strengthen your brothers." - Luke
22:31-32 (NLT)*

Introduction

This chapter discusses how individual
prayer assignments can come with a
Spirit-given tenderness for specific people
within the categories of Jews, the Nations, or the
Church. It explores how the Holy Spirit prompts
us to pray for individuals, just as Jesus prayed for
Peter.

Word of Wisdom

"The Holy Spirit will alert you to

someone's needs. Keep in mind that if what you perceive about a person makes you critical of them, the one who has made you aware of the area of weakness is not the Holy Spirit."

Main Theme

Understanding and responding to God's promptings to pray for specific individuals, recognizing these as divine assignments that require sensitivity and obedience.

Key Points

• The Holy Spirit can give a tenderness in your heart for an individual, prompting you to pray.

• Jesus prayed for Peter, showing how prayer can strengthen someone in their time of need.

• The Holy Spirit will alert you to someone's needs, not to criticize but to intercede.

• God often brings individuals to your attention to prompt prayer.

• Simple remembrance of someone can be a prompt from the Holy Spirit.

Key Themes

- **Spirit-Given Tenderness:** The Holy Spirit can place a special tenderness in our hearts for individuals, prompting us to pray for them with compassion and sensitivity. This tenderness is a divine indication of a prayer assignment.

- **Jesus' Example with Peter:** Jesus' prayer for Peter serves as a model for intercessory prayer. He prayed for Peter's faith not to fail, demonstrating that our prayers can support others through their weaknesses and challenges.
- **Responding to the Holy Spirit:** When the Holy Spirit brings someone to our attention, it is a divine prompting to pray. This can be as simple as remembering someone and lifting them up in prayer, allowing God to work through our obedience.
- **Supernatural in the Natural:** Promptings to pray often seem natural but have supernatural significance. Even a simple memory of someone can be a divine call to intercession, leading to powerful spiritual outcomes.
- **Reporting to God:** Just as nerves in the body report pain to the brain, we report our prayer promptings to God. We don't need to know everything; our role is to return to God in prayer what He gives us, allowing Him to activate the necessary help.

Conclusion

By responding to the Holy Spirit's promptings to pray for individuals, we participate in God's work on earth. These seemingly small acts of obedience can have significant spiritual impacts, as we align ourselves with God's purposes and intercede for those He places on our hearts. Like Jesus, our lives can reflect the works of God as we respond faithfully to His prompts.

CHAPTER 27

CONTEND FOR THE DESTINIES

Bible Verse

"I appeal to you [I entreat you], brethren, for the sake of our Lord Jesus Christ and by the love [given by] the Spirit, to unite with me in earnest wrestling in prayer to God in my behalf." - Romans 15:30 (AMPC)

Introduction

This chapter explores the importance of contending in prayer for the destinies of individuals. It highlights how personal prayer assignments can shift from one immediate concern to a broader intercession for the destinies of many.

Word of Wisdom

"The fulfilling of every detail pertaining to a purpose of God is the undoing

of plans and purposes in the kingdom of darkness."

Main Theme

Recognizing and responding to the Holy Spirit's call to contend in prayer for the destinies of individuals, understanding that these assignments are critical in God's overarching plan.

Key Points

• Contending for destinies involves shifting prayer focus from immediate concerns to broader intercession.

• David's prayers for his first child may have also impacted the destiny of Solomon.

• The devil targets destinies that threaten his kingdom, as seen in biblical accounts.

• Paul frequently requested prayer for his protection and mission due to the contention over his destiny.

• Prophetic words and scriptures serve as weapons in contending for destinies.

Key Themes

• **Shifting Prayer Focus:** The author shares an experience of praying for a baby and realizing the broader scope of praying for multiple destinies. This shift in focus highlights the importance of being open to the Holy Spirit's guidance in prayer.

- **Biblical Examples of Contention:** The chapter examines biblical stories where the devil targeted individuals' destinies, such as Moses and Jesus. These stories illustrate the intense spiritual battles over significant destinies.

- **Paul's Prayer Requests:** Paul often asked for prayers from the churches, understanding the spiritual contention over his mission. His letters demonstrate the importance of communal prayer support for those with significant callings.

- **Role of Prophetic Words:** Prophetic words provide clarity and focus for intercessory prayer. They serve as divine insight into God's plans for individuals, helping believers to pray effectively for their destinies.

- **Obedience and Alignment:** Obedience to God's instructions in prayer assignments aligns individuals with His purposes. This obedience not only impacts the person being prayed for but also brings personal spiritual growth and transformation.

Conclusion

Contending for the destinies of individuals is a crucial aspect of intercessory prayer. By responding to the Holy Spirit's prompts and using prophetic words and scriptures, believers can effectively participate in God's plan. This obedience and alignment with God's purposes lead to significant spiritual outcomes for both the intercessor and those they pray for. Through diligent and faithful prayer, we partner with God in fulfilling His divine purposes.

❧

CHAPTER 28

TIMES AND SEASONS

Bible Verse

"The Lord will not abandon his people, because that would dishonor his great name. For it has pleased the Lord to make you his very own people." - 1 Samuel 12:22 (NLT)

Introduction

This chapter delves into the various durations and types of prayer assignments seen throughout the Bible. Understanding these examples helps believers recognize and respond to God's promptings for prayer, ensuring they participate effectively in God's plans.

Word of Wisdom

"Recognizing aspects of the various assignments can certainly help us not miss them but instead participate with God."

Main Theme

Understanding the diverse durations and natures of prayer assignments in the Bible and learning to respond appropriately to the Holy Spirit's promptings.

Key Points

• Prayer assignments vary greatly in duration, from brief moments to lifelong commitments.

• Abram's prayer for Sodom and Gomorrah may have been brief or extended over days.

• Moses' intercession for Israel was a lifelong assignment, marked by multiple critical intercessions.

• Samuel committed to praying for Israel continuously, regardless of their actions.

• Ezra's prayer for the returning Jews involved deep repentance and intercession.

• Daniel's prayers spanned his entire life, influencing nations and future events.

• Anna and Simeon devoted their lives to praying for the Messiah's arrival.

Key Themes

• **Abram and Sodom and Gomorrah:**
  Abram's intercession for Sodom and
  Gomorrah was a divinely initiated,
  potentially brief but impactful prayer,
  highlighting the importance of interceding
  for those we are connected to.

- **Moses and Israel:** Moses' prayer assignment for Israel was ongoing and multifaceted, demonstrating how long-term intercession can be integral to fulfilling God's purposes for a group of people.
- **Samuel's Commitment:** Samuel's dedication to praying for Israel shows that prayer assignments can be lifelong commitments, rooted in our relationship with God rather than the gratitude or recognition of those we pray for.
- **Ezra's Intercession:** Ezra's prayer for the Jews returning from Babylon involved identifying with their sins and seeking God's mercy, illustrating how deep repentance and intercession are vital in restoring God's people.
- **Daniel's Lifelong Prayer:** Daniel's prayer life spanned multiple regimes and included fasting, demonstrating the power of sustained, faithful prayer in bringing about God's purposes on a global scale.

Conclusion

Understanding the different types and durations of prayer assignments helps believers respond effectively to God's promptings. These assignments are not about the length or intensity of the prayer but about faithfulness and obedience to God's call. Recognizing and embracing these assignments allows us to participate in God's plans, influencing individuals, nations, and the unfolding of His purposes.

CHAPTER 29

THE SOVIET UNION

Bible Verse

"The earnest (heartfelt, continued) prayer of a righteous man makes tremendous power available [dynamic in its working]." - James 5:16b (AMPC)

Introduction

T his chapter recounts the spiritual journey and powerful prayers that contributed to the unexpected dissolution of the Soviet Union. It highlights how dedicated, Spirit-led intercession can influence global events and change the course of history.

Word of Wisdom

"Relinquish your need to pray from your own understanding, efforts, and agenda, and instead work with God."

Main Theme

The supernatural impact of persistent, Spirit-directed prayer on the dissolution of the Soviet Union, demonstrating the power of partnering with God in prayer.

Key Points

• The Soviet Union, a formidable superpower, existed from 1922–1991, oppressing religion and personal freedoms.

• During the Cold War, prayer groups worldwide, including a group led by Kenneth E. Hagin, prayed fervently for the Soviet Union.

• Spirit-led prayer, using scriptures as a foundation, played a crucial role in the Soviet Union's dissolution.

• Mikhail Gorbachev's rise to power and subsequent reforms were influenced by divine intervention and prayer.

• The collapse of the Soviet Union led to unprecedented religious freedom and the spread of the gospel in previously closed nations.

• Prayer's role in global events underscores the importance of relying on the Holy Spirit for guidance and direction.

Key Themes

- **Historical Context:** The Soviet Union was a significant global power that oppressed religious freedom and individual rights. Its dissolution was a complex event influenced by various factors, including prayer.

- **Power of Spirit-Led Prayer:** Kenneth E. Hagin's group prayed persistently using specific scriptures, demonstrating how targeted, scriptural prayer can align with God's will and bring about significant change.
- **Mikhail Gorbachev's Role:** Gorbachev, unlike previous leaders, showed genuine care for the people, leading to reforms that eventually dismantled the Soviet Union. His leadership was part of God's plan, influenced by the prayers of the faithful.
- **Supernatural Transformation:** The peaceful collapse of the Soviet Union and the subsequent religious freedom were supernatural events that cannot be attributed solely to political actions. This transformation was a result of divine intervention through prayer.
- **Impact on the Gospel:** The fall of the Soviet Union opened doors for thousands of ministers to spread the gospel in previously restricted areas, showcasing the far-reaching effects of answered prayers.

Conclusion

The story of the Soviet Union's dissolution illustrates the tremendous power of Spirit-led prayer in influencing global events. By partnering with God in prayer, believers can participate in His divine plans and witness miraculous changes. This chapter encourages readers to engage in persistent, faith-filled prayer, trusting in God's sovereignty and timing.

Harrison House is a Spirit-filled, Word of Faith Christian publisher dedicated to spreading the message of faith, hope, and love through our wide range of inspiring publications. Committed to the messages that highlight the power of the Word and Spirit, we provide books, devotionals, and study guides that empower believers to live victorious, faith-filled lives.

Our resources are designed to help readers grow spiritually, strengthen their faith, and experience the transformative power of God's Word. Harrison House is passionate about equipping Christians with the tools they need to fulfill their divine purpose and impact the world for Christ.

www.ingramcontent.com/pod-product-compliance
Lightning Source LLC
Chambersburg PA
CBHW051431090426
42737CB00014B/2911